PENGUIN B

Ceremony for th

CW00545624

Theresa Lola is a British Nigerian poe
the Young People's Laureate for London in the year 2019–20. In 2018
she was awarded the Brunel International African Poetry Prize. She
holds a Master's in Creative Writing from University of Oxford. In
2022 the poem 'Equilibrium' from her debut poetry collection, *In
Search of Equilibrium*, was added to OCR's GCSE English Literature
syllabus.

THERESA LOLA

Ceremony for the Nameless

PENGUIN BOOKS

PENGUIN BOOKS

UK | USA | Canada | Ireland | Australia
India | New Zealand | South Africa

Penguin Books is part of the Penguin Random House group of companies
whose addresses can be found at global.penguinrandomhouse.com

First published in Penguin Books 2024

001

Set in 9.75/13.5pt Warnock Pro
Typeset by Jouve (UK), Milton Keynes
Printed and bound in Great Britain by Clays Ltd, Elcograf S.p.A.

The authorized representative in the EEA is Penguin Random House Ireland,
Morrison Chambers, 32 Nassau Street, Dublin D02 YH68

A CIP catalogue record for this book is available from the British Library

ISBN: 978–1–802–06579–4

www.greenpenguin.co.uk

CONTENTS

To live is to have a name;
to have a name is to live.

Niyi Osundare

Name 1
All repeat *Name 1*

Name 2
All repeat *Name 2*

Name 3
All repeat *Name 3*

Name 4
All repeat *Name 4*

Name 5
All repeat *Name 5*

Surname
All repeat *Surname*

Chorus at the Ceremony

Your babied mouth can't join the choir yet
but you feel the ribbon of sounds on your cheeks.
By the repetition of your third name,
our breaths are in sync.
With the chanting of your fifth name,
our hearts lilt in sync.
Angelic dancers, unseen by the surface eye,
silk in our midst.
We instil your names into the air, as if to say,
a molecule must register your melody.

Your eyes swirl over the various shapes of grace.
Family is a circus of fanciful contentions.
This is a ceremony of your becoming,
and – permit us – a ceremony of our binding.
Today we give thanks for all your names,
for the harmony they make of our bodies.
Our dear, when your teeth grow strong
enough, join us, sing with us.
Store the spine of this day in your heart.
A necklace of names for one.

Let this not be in vain.

First Miracle I Witnessed

Let them be ashamed and brought to mutual confusion
Who seek to destroy my life.

   Psalm 40:14

A bedroom window shattered
and a naked terror emerged.
Thieves swept our house with guns.
My mother grabbed her three children,
hid us in the first place she could find:

a cupboard with netted doors.
It concealed nothing, made us feel naked.
Our teeth shook against their roots
and my mother uttered silent prayers,
different from her morning ones.

God deliver us from our fellow men.
The thieves walked in our direction,
guided by hunger,
their faces naked of conscience.
They wanted money, money, money.

The thieves searched for our faces –
they looked at us, looked inside us,
then looked past us, walked past us.
Did they see us? How didn't they see us?
A pause. Nothing. Seized by confusion,

the thieves bolted out.
Next morning, we found a fallen baseball cap.
The words on it read 'God Bless You'.
My mother unravelled praises to whom
she called Jehovah Nissi, God her protector.

I'd heard of His many names. Now for the first time
I *knew* this one's nature: knew the God who covers nakedness.
A dreadful question nearly stripped me of my awe –
If miracles are attached to anguish,
how will I come to encounter God's *other* names?

My Name Is My Home

Ilé l'à á wò kí a tó sọ ọmọ l'órúko. ('You do not name a child unless you know the condition of the home into which they are born.')

Yoruba proverb

Every time someone mispronounces my name
they break its windows, dirty the floors,
replace things, take things.

In a secondary school in Bromley my Yoruba name
pronounced Foon-mi is bent into Fun-mi,
and so are the house rules.

They enter my name with a litter of confetti.
In a different school a girl calls me Fanny,
claims it sounds similar.

I don't resist. Watch her strip clothes from my room.
Her small hands splinter my wardrobe
back to a wooden idea.

In another school
I remove the 'n' in the spelling of my name, mistake
what is subtle for what is silent.

Go by Fumi instead of Funmi.
Then I remember what the letter *n* means to my skin folk,
the weapon-shaped word it carries.

so I grab the *n* back, and feel
the roof inside my name reposition itself.
At university I switch

to my middle name. But graduation reveals our full names,
makes sure our true selves are awarded. On this day
my full name, Olufunmilola (Olu-foon-mi-lola), meaning

Olú – God
    fún – given
        mi – me *olá* – wealth

is twisted into Olu-funny-ola
by a lecturer. The staircase
inside my name flattens into a trampoline,

alters the way my prayers reach for height.
Every time someone mispronounces my name
they disrupt its foundations.

Replace things. Break things.
Now, I'm left with no choice but to build spiked gates,
position armed guards. I must shield my name.

Carousel of Oil Sheen

Fine ghel do you want to do your hair?
The hairdresser asked when I entered the salon.
The air was a carousel of oil sheen.
This is the script of Lagos.
What else is hair for if not to shine shine and shake
like shekere and tambourine?
The hairdresser said to me
after I mapped out the elaborate hairstyle I wanted.
When someone asked to jump the queue
she called, *Give me five minutes, please.*
She was a full-time scientist of time.
People came in to buy bags, clothes, shoes, everything.
She put a blob of Blue Magic on the back of her hand;
her eyes deftly measured it. Then
she drew a line through my scalp with an ilarun.
A phone was sandwiched between her ear and shoulder,
I eavesdropped on her chats –
her words flowed like therapy pulp.
When I moved to London,
I found a hairdresser in Woolwich,
wondering if small mirrors can reflect a previous life.

Wondering if small mirrors can reflect a previous life,
I found a hairdresser in Woolwich
when I moved to London.
Her words flowed like therapy pulp.
I eavesdropped on her chats –
a phone was sandwiched between her ear and shoulder.
She drew a line through my scalp with an ilarun;
her eyes deftly measured it. Then
she put a blob of Blue Magic on the back of her hand.
People came in to buy bags, clothes, shoes, everything.
She was a full-time scientist of time.
she called, *Give me five minutes, please,*
when someone asked to jump the queue.
After I mapped out the elaborate hairstyle I wanted
the hairdresser said to me
Like shekere and tambourine,
what else is hair for if not to shine shine and shake.
This is the script of Lagos.
The air was a carousel of oil sheen.
When I entered the salon the hairdresser asked,
Fine ghel do you want to do your hair?

Tracing My Colour

Instead of orange
    we Yoruba say
the colour of the liquid from inside an orange.

Instead of blue,
    we say the colour that emerges
by crushing elu leaves,
    mixing them with soda and water,
soaking them till they turn into
what our hands can make art with.

I want to dive into the body of the earth,
to be lathered with its saliva,
to hear the soundscape of its bones,
to sleep upon the meat in its belly. I want

more. What is colour
if not an opening into this world of surprises?

The art teacher asks us which colours make brown,
and we twirl brushes into a row of acrylic paints.
Some say yellow + blue + red.
Others say red + green.
Also, blue + orange. I am bored by the answers.

I put my hand up. I say, *Imagine*
if green leaves were crushed,
mixed with soda + water to form what you call blue.
Then pour orange juice into it.
It will produce the colour you wonder about.

Brown is a shorthand word
for what makes the sky and sun shiver in delight.

Oríkì for the Migrant

Yours was a difficult birth,
the air fibrous and fidgety.
Gather tales of your entrance –
map your galaxy of scars.

Know that
the earth prayed for you to rise
from one of its seeds.
Your lineage is cassava,
is food for generations
and generations and generations.

Migrant!
Did you know God gave you the hope
to withstand the madness of labyrinths?
You are the great-great-granddaughter
of one who stirred the fibres of the forest
into a ceremonial garment.

Curious creature,
while others played hide-and-seek
you sought the wind through winding roads.

Migrant!
The one who writes of this world.
Why do you think God gave you the gift
to withstand the madness of labyrinths?
He knew you
while you were a still a thought
searching the womb.
He set apart your inheritance.

Migrant! Fluent street-food speaker.
Many have asked, *where is your home office?*
They want to know how you built that mansion
on the hill of your restless head.

Here Stand before Us the North and South

In 1897 Flora Shaw first coined the term 'Nigeria' in an essay
referring to what was then the British protectorate.
In 1900 the protectorates were made up of Northern Nigeria
and Southern Nigeria. In 1902 colonial administrator
Frederick Lugard married Flora Shaw. In 1914 he became
governor of both territories and amalgamated the
two protectorates into what he termed Nigeria.

The North and South stood at the altar,
unveiled, jittery in unironed suits.

Lord and Lady Lugard, the officiators,
said *speak now or forever hold your peace.*

This is the part where the congregation should
have slathered the aisle with laughter.

The silenced have scant peace to hold;
the remnants suffocate in their closed fists.

Lord and Lady Lugard
thought of the union after they too

had won each other's hearts,
desired the same for the couple before them.

How kind to be led by example.
Two is better than one,

for *they* get a good return for *their* labour.
The North and South

left the aisle newly addressed as Nigeria.
Lord and Lady Lugard led by example,

not until death did they part – As for Nigeria,
many meddled in their marriage.

Still, they went on to birth children.
Of which I am one.

Our parents argue so often
the curtains haven't been changed

for a while now.
The compound is large and airy,

in need of family albums and quirky trays,
in need of warmth, not dull heat.

Opposites may attract, but our differences
are both compass and encompassing.

We the children shoot our heads out
of the window, glare at multiple horizons.

Maybe we daydream too much. Imagining
the day our parents will renew their vows.

Our Appellations: Orúkọ Àbísọ

General generous! We welcome you.
You were the first to arrive bearing gifts:
new honour, a victory sign, ordained wealth.
Your next of kin are here to festoon you
with names in response.
The first name presented is Olufunmilola.

[redacted]

HISTORY TEACHER: Fela Kuti's mother
was the first woman in Nigeria to drive a car.

STUDENTS: Mr [redacted], where was she headed?

HISTORY TEACHER: She was just traversing roads.

STUDENTS: But to where?

HISTORY TEACHER: To Alake's palace.
The back seat was crammed with women.
A few sat in the boot.

STUDENTS: Why were they going there?

HISTORY TEACHER: To sing abusive at the king.
Brooms were clutched in their hands,
their stalks flared out like trumpets.

STUDENTS: Why?

HISTORY TEACHER: Because life was taxing.

STUDENTS: What about the men?

HISTORY TEACHER: I meant to say
the tax was heavier on women.
They chorused curses on the king
and his colonial lord.

STUDENTS: What's the name of the woman
who led this revolt? Fela's mother.

HISTORY TEACHER: Good question.
I don't have that in my notes. Wait.
Ahh, turns out she's my wife's namesake!

STUDENTS: . . . and her name, sir?

HISTORY TEACHER: Funmilayo Ransome-Kuti.

Song for My Mother Dancing in Front of the Mirror in Our Room

My mother is dancing in front of the mirror
in our room. We spread a bedsheet
of praise, for the day we never doubted or betrayed
is here. My sister and I flock to my mother,
bring pointed heels, a bracelet, plum lipstick,
gold-plated earrings, sambac jasmine perfume.
Her eye bags are still present,
but minutes of relief have subdued them.
We hail her, *Ghenghencious!*
This road must clear for you!
Her tall and thick exam books are sat
by the windowsill, still as salty spectators.

> When we grow past these concrete walls
> may we still adorn you like it's our call.
> Shivering bird, plastic sky, summer or spring,
> may time dream of trumpets when we sing.

My mother tugs off the dress price tag
like a cork from a champagne bottle.
A toast to winning the campaign for a new start,
our voices vibrant as fireworks.
A toast to thriving despite bladed borders.
We dance without added music: all the songs
are bound as bone inside us. We swirl and bend
till the wind is dizzy from watching,
till our smiles are miles longer than before,
and a hope ripples inside us.
We grip our reflection in the mirror,
take in what lies behind.

When we grow past these concrete walls
may we still adorn you like it's our call.
Shivering bird, plastic sky, summer or spring,
may time dream of trumpets when we sing.

In a few years we'll gather by the mirror again.
Me in my creamy billowing wedding dress.
My mother will zip my corset, show me
a loose thread of homesickness.
Her nails are soft-gel red.
My sister will study the reflection, and poof she sees
many visions, like what hairstyle fits best.
We'll find ways to keep looking at each other,
reminisce about the years spent searching
for a home with a large mirror.
We only wish for the other to be seen
as time carries us into wherever we next call home.

When we grow past these concrete walls
may we still adorn you like it's our call.
Shivering bird, plastic sky, summer or spring,
may time dream of trumpets when we sing.

Citizenship Ceremony, 2012

Dear highly skilled migrant,
according to our Home Office you have
enough points to proceed with your life.
We are gathered here this bright afternoon
to present your body before a photograph
of Our Majesty the Queen, and before God.
Old borders have passed away;
all bothers have become new.
Now repeat after me:
I do solemnly promise to be noble, grateful,
a faithful living sacrifice, kind to dogs,
obsessed with the weather,
to know Ofcom's telephone number by heart,
to sing (sincerely) 'It's Coming Home'
at each World Cup with my doors open
yearning for a lick of the trophy
at my registered address. – So help me God.
Now we invite you to chorus
the National Anthem with us.
Dear newly certified British citizen,
I hope you soaked in the past thirty minutes.
I guess those years of stacking cardboard
in a dark room have paid off.

The Interviewer Asks What I Do in My Spare Time

I practise how to say *hire me* in a tone that isn't overt.
I buy purple lipstick then realise I meant plum or lilac.
There are no refunds on certain products. I know risk.

I'm terrible at impressions, but I have a gift for imagining
I'm you wearing a crisp shirt soiled with starch
Googling names of applicants while eating Walkers crisps.

In my spare time I pour bleach over my internet fingerprints.
A student of *CSI Miami, NY, Cyber.* Some missing people
turn up years later on the internet bearing their 'artist' name.

There's a takeaway by the roundabout on the way here.
I love cooking. Hire me and I'll bring packed lunches,
present it to you all in exchange for a new adjective.

That's all I know about working in an office.
In the mirror I say mad things and claim they are poems.
I strum my ribs in honour of music. Have you tried it?

The body is a blabber – there's so much to listen to.
Hire me, pay my light bills so I can think clearly.
For you, I'll be completely sane.

Greeting the Elders

I pop into the supermarket
on the way home from work.
I'm walking past the meat aisle
when I see an old family friend.
Hi Liz, I utter so fast
my own gasp startles the air.

Who are you calling Liz?
She sparks.

I was unprepared for this.

My body is still inside an office,
participating in a festival of handshakes
and first names.

I genuflect. *Ssssorry, Aunty* I plead,
but I dragged out the S too long
I feel a snake in my throat.
She shrugs, grabs a steak from the fridge
and leaves.

I must not forget what I was taught as a child:
that with age a name becomes a guarded mystery.
We pronounce a title instead,
all its fat in our mouth.

Why does the red liquid that drips from meat
look so much like blood?
I must remember that it isn't.
There's a culture that travels through it.
For the body, it does some good.

Our Appellations: Orúkọ Àmútọ̀runwá

Alternative birth story. After I emerge
my mother gives birth again, this time to a mirror.
She calls her Kehinde. I'm given Taiwo.
When I introduce myself, they ask of her.
When she introduces herself, they ask of me.
She'll say her sister is a writer.
She'll say she is an accountant.
She'll say she does my taxes.
She'll vouch that I pay my taxes.
She'll promise that we aren't that different;
we both keep ledgers on people's lives,
we both can manipulate reality.
Some nights, snacking on salted cashew nuts,
we jokingly recount how for years we wished
the other would just disappear.
We accept that time was meant to unfold this way.
Like the pairing of lightning and thunder;
how the veins of light appear first,
before the resounding applause arrives.

Nocturnal Migrant
after Chip

Who are you?
Legs of a nosy tourist,
gulping *grime*
gas.

        raver

            eater

        streeter
in a wool *jumper.*
You're carrying a bottle of
Lyrical

            chlorine
taken from the top shelf
of a double decker bus.
You gurgle the words,
spit it onto a mirror,
clean your accent

        raw to da corer.
Since landing in Heathrow
have you slept?
Every socket in your body
is testing new switches.
Electric tongued music.
Who are you?
You will say

        grime
only.
Don't forget you were already

a brilliant kind of dirt.
Who are you?
You ask me.
look, by now u kno da name.

Language Is a Road of Desire

My language is a road paved on my tongue.
My Yoruba teacher applauded me in class.
This is untrue, but this lie is my loudest song.

I have laid subgrades of words since I was young.
Sleeves rolled, I learned from the adults at work.
My language is a road paved on my tongue.

By the texture of speech I know I belong:
feel the grit of my accent, its various tones.
This is untrue, but this lie is my loudest song.

Things that can reshape the road, I have flung
into the abyss of the bush, to ensure
my language remains a road paved on my tongue.

Ask me any question, test if I am wrong.
Preferably at night, under dim streetlights.
My language is a road paved on my tongue.
This is untrue, but this lie is my loudest song.

My Names Converse

OLUFUNMILOLA: You don't want to be seen in public with me anymore. I'm too much for you, aren't I?

THERESA LOLA: I have taken the 'lola' from you as a souvenir, to remember the wealth of who you are. Even elevated it to a stand-alone word.

OLUFUNMILOLA: Spare me the boredom. You children of the diaspora, you like to dangle a portion of your heritage as bait.

THERESA LOLA: Don't be so difficult.

OLUFUNMILOLA: Let's hope you aren't the one that gets eaten.

What a Party It Was

The name-droppers were dropping dead & the party went on.
Waiters served elderflower in used glasses,
old lipstick prints still visible on the rims.
They had no time to wash trivial things like cutlery.

We had been dancing for years: our sores gave birth to sores.
We belted out songs we'd known all our lives
& ones we learned seconds before. This was a party
& a celebrity was in attendance. A celebrity was in attendance.

We felt no urge to go home, even though there was no bed
comfortable enough to sleep on. & as for food,
flies fellowshipped on shifting plates of slow-cooked lamb.
In there, our bodies were different; we didn't care:

our stomachs felt fuller from chaos than from bread.
The dead bodies began to smell, and the celebrity led us
in moving them to a locked room. We tried to keep dancing,
but some grew weak, or bored, some sick, others sickened.

A pen is somewhere exhausted from the NDAs we signed.
Our celebrity was afraid we would speak of this.
But deep down, more afraid no one would ever
desire to dance with them, or for them.

These days we speak of the celebrity like an unmarked grave.
We own their skeletons. There was a silent agreement
it was never theirs to begin with. And nor was their name,
but they had enough money to lease that back from us.

Closing Ceremony

The day has come. The office of life has crumbled.

The ground that was yawning from exhaustion

has remained open,

a kind of relief only the dead show.

Coal no longer rises to attend staff meetings.

A tiger naps by a lake with a tattered suit on.

Robots have developed anaemia.

Houses have run off to console the sea, their slaughtered lover.

We remember trees by the gnarled veins in our purple legs.

I hold my husband; hold our children,

whose small eyes question. We pretend

this is the set of a film daddy is making.

We the survivors, for lack of better words,

are sat uncomfortably on mauled mountains,

    huddle like cavemen as we share

    our findings from the ashes left,

test what things we can make from them.

Being labourers is all we know, is the fulcrum of our lot.

Even when the earth retreats back to void,

our addiction to stripping it remains.

We have an affinity with nakedness.

For we are born naked, and return to our maker naked.

My Hair Is Due

Your hair is due
my hairdresser said.
By due she meant due
for a creamy pay, due
to be liberated
from nature's errors, due
to no longer have
bladed strings
disguised as curls.

Your hair is due.
She stopped the sentence here –
I knew the relaxer's bite
on my scalp would be the full stop.
I was sat on the chair,
sweaty and sheepish.
Then, I remembered
the girl in boarding school
whose hair

was so stubborn
it kicked a comb in the stomach.
We groaned in disbelief.
Wondered what secret wealth
she owned, what made her dare
reject what we were told
we were owed.
I know now. It was the realisation
that humans are crafty,

we reframe words to contain
more than appears. At the ninth hour,
as the hairdresser parted
my scabbed scalp
an awakening arrived.
I yanked the comb. Jolted up.
Never looked back.
Now when I say due, I mean,
a time for what I desire.

Ceremony

Wise women and men arrive bearing gifts.
Honey, salt, palm oil, alligator pepper:
each adds its flavour to your appointed name.

They profess they will eat from it someday
and boast that the future was worth hoping for.
It takes a village to raise a child, and

now you are a teenager. Every street you turn
there is a villager bearing eyes and proverbs.
They remind you of the alligator pepper

which has brown seeds vast as the stars.
They declare that your descendants too will be
like stars descended and dyed brown.

At sixteen you announce you will become an optometrist.
Last year you were called to be an architect.
The year before you believed an orchestra lived inside you.

Now you are twenty-eight, still with vague purpose.
The villagers ask when they can come to feast,
speak with a twang of impatience, like they are owed a taste.

Maybe that's an unfair thought. One of many you have.
Your mind is as shrivelled as an alligator pepper's skin,
frustrated by your reality's blandness.

You begin again. New recipes, old prophecies.
You were welcomed into the world with a ceremony,
and have spent your life seeking the return of an audience.

You are slowly realising you have to concern yourself less with expectations. Care first about the taste of your name in your own mouth.

My Middle Name Returns from Work

She gathers her hair, a field of ripe black crops,
lips lined in nineties coffee brown.
She strides silkier in heels than my first name does.
She pays all the rent,

lives at the confluence of income streams.
She knows of harvest, her hands innately deft.
My middle name was known in this continent,
dare I say beloved, years before I was wombed.

The first of her kind was Therasia from Spain,
a fourth-century Christian aristocrat.
I jest, remind my middle name that my first name
translates to 'God has given me wealth.'

She too could have fended for us.
My middle name shrugs & gowns away.
In France she is known as Thérèse of Lisieux,
nicknamed *little flower*:

a thing to be looked after.
A friend's mother once said to me,
Saint Teresa, pray for us that our barns may be full.
Her chuckle enveloped her body.

My middle name knows her etymology
is a row of Greek symbols: θερίζω.
She poses as rockstar, rubs shoulders
with the artist formerly known as Prince.

After removing her work shoes,
I advise my middle name to take tomorrow off.
I invite her & my first name to the dining room
to sit, eat & laugh like a family with no favourites.

While we wait
I rub my first name's back,
massage the notes on her flat spine.
Her smile languishing by the minute.

My middle name hesitates, then joins us.
We try . . . but conversations falter.
There has been too much distance.
We no longer know what makes the other laugh.

Burial for the Unceremoniously Buried

In 2009 excavation works uncovered a mass grave in Valle da Gafaria,
Portugal. There were skeletons of over 150 enslaved Africans.
Most had been dumped. Some had their feet and hands bound.
The site has since been covered by a parking lot and a mini golf course.

It is the middle of the night.
We are gathered at a mini golf course
in Lagos (Portugal).
We are allocated pieces of green land,
disperse in groups to gouge them out.
Beneath this playground of cavities
lie piles of dormant teeth.
Our ancestors are not dead, just waiting
to be moved to a comfortable bed.
Finally. The ground gives up
all hundredandfiftyeight of you.
We untie your hands and
hear an ensemble of skeletal sighs.
We anoint each worthy bone
with fat. Massage your tense skulls.
Dust the earth from your phalanges.
We take turns to pray in languages
that nearly died with you.
One by one, we carry you gently
into the convoy of caskets,
into a good night.
Forgive this mass address;
there are no passports, no diaries,
no phone books, no birth certificates,
no nosy neighbours to call.
This day was strategically planned,
but still, tears are jumping the queue.

The moon is tilting its head to watch.
The wind keeps loudly begging
for forgiveness, confesses how
it was hired to shift your foul smell.
We close the last casket,
and a thought unlatches in our chests.
Will there ever be a right place
to rebury you?

Bird Catching

I tell my mother I want
to ditch my dream
of becoming a writer.
Claim it would be easy.
All I have to do is recall
my invention from the sky:
a human that can fly,
half-beak, half-bum.
No one finds birds interesting
anymore. They appear
in too many poems.
Problem is my invention
now has a mind of its own.
It is refusing to return.
I look up how to trap a bird –
surely the same rules apply.
I would need an animal carcass,
perhaps a dead catfish,
or a rope, or a rocket net.
My mother thinks it's so much
trouble to contain this thing,
that I'm leading my pain astray.
All this energy could be spent
developing my human bird,
sharpening its eyesight,
fattening its stamina.
Holed up in my messy room,
skin dry and dirty,
I remember that I migrated here
with a suitcase of carcass.
A heavy bag of memories
that a strange bird could eat.

I open it and in a blink
my human bird returns to feast.
The urge to kidnap it halts.
Instead, I gaze at it,
awed like a mad scientist.
I've never seen it enjoy
a meal this much.

Nakedness

I am told I should just create a name, spit it into dust and knead.
How do people hold theirs with such certainty? If only I could sneak
into their skin. I envy them, resent my neediness, my needs.
At times I exit my body, a need to distance from the dankness
inside me, from the cold and fear, the shivering at the knees.
Without a name I am an unverified existence. All I seek
snakes away; a home, a bank account, a passport, a living, *ease.*
At least in death I will be granted a name, 'Jane Doe.' All this ends.
Thank the human need to give a noun to discovery, to make sense
of it, of us. My skull, a forensic playground on a detective's desk.
I might be dead, but I will be flattered to be named. Seen.

Ghazal for the Nostalgic

Return to the past with buckets, press oil from your memories.
Grip the shiny gems and glow up with oil from your memories.

Small with a shaky poise, resist a fierce desire for closure:
pressing the past with desperate speed will spoil all memories.

Bless the small brutalities of Bebo, MSN, Yahoo.
Hold the naive heat of youth and wrap foil on the memories.

Double dutch over borders, you exist between here and there.
When injury flares up, lance the boil, push through the memories.

Some recollections might differ: your brain is a risky source.
If you searched your sly self, you would recoil from some memories.

You are a writer, Theresa, all journeys are eventful.
Seek the potholes and be ready to toil in the memories.

Grandma Says She Is Dying

Over the phone my grandma says she is dying, she is dying.
I almost forget her name.
When she says my name, she cradles its brittle neck;
her voice is trumpet-full.

How are you, Grandma?

I am fine, how are you, dear?

I'm fine, too – fine as in, I'm still practising
your trumpet laugh, Grandma.
What are you dying of, Grandma?

Old age. Anyway, how is England?

It's cold, Grandma, as in: my fingers feel like consonants.
How's Nigeria?

*It is hot, my dear, as in: sweat rushes like vowels.
When are you visiting me in Nigeria?*

I promise I will before your day of dying.
We'll dance to a trumpet playing,
wash our head with what bursts from its funnel.

OK, dear, and how is your master's going?

It's going, Grandma, I'm mastering how to hold a poem
the way a trumpet is held; with hands, with mouth,
with the whole body, without dying.
I'm mastering how to write
the way a trumpet stretches a map of sounds
from only three notes, doesn't give room for dying.

Well done, I hope you are being a good older sister?

I'm trying: teaching them to cradle daily vowels,
telling them of life's consonants.

I'm proud of you, my dear. Here's a prayer for you:
hook it to your ears when you think of dying.
Àmín ni oruko Jésù.

Grandma, how have you kept your strength taut,
still pressing the valve of your prayers?

Well, my dear, I believe a prayer is a poem,
except God is the ghost writer.
That's one last excitement of being alive:
wondering what God will create
each time I open my mouth.
My love for God is far from brittle,
                    far from dying.

To the Man Who Called Me a Black Bastard
While I Was on My Way to Church

Which was the greater insult, being black, or being a bastard? I need
to streamline my war. My pastor advised us to ease our exhausted
guardian angels. Which was the greater insult, being black, or being
a bastard? Here is a photo of my parents on their wedding day. Look
my father in the eye through his oversized glasses and pitch him
your fiction. Part of your diagnosis is true. I am black. I remained
black even after being scrubbed anew by God. In the bathtub I
learned black bastards too are fathered by God. I saw feathers drop-
ping from your mouth. There is a word for people like you, those
who hunt down other people's guardian angels and eat their wings.

Somewhere There Is an Opening

Each visitor is an extra mouth uttering, calling,
gathering this building's name into a casual chant.
Instantly Edward Colston is summoned. He appears
before a number of us, holding pieces of marred
flesh, taunting us with all the dead that did not make
it. We rock our stomach in its own vomit, run to the
antiseptic hallway, and ask the strolling visitors if
they saw him too, urge *them* to help us uncurse this
building, cast out its name. They laugh, say ghosts
aren't real. Then tell us dreams they had as a child
of ghosts replacing their white bones with white
strings and yanking them out of bed. 'See, it's just the
mind's fantasy!' they say. We chant 'Bloody Mary' in
a reggae of rage right in their face. And they begin
squirming, seizing their skin with their hands, as
if terrified of being dismantled. It all makes non-
sense. The man does not appear to them because
he lives inside them – I hear the visitors in the hall
grumbling, wondering why the concert break is
taking so long. They just want to see us perform,
brittle or Bristol. They desire riffs to make them
remember beauty, or to make them forget that it's
raining blood but somehow the roof isn't leaking.

Olive and Clement

In 1969 Olive Morris was beaten by a police officer
after intervening in the arrest of Clement Gomwalk
outside a record shop in Brixton.

Olive and Clement
enter a record shop in Brixton,
seeking to sing something
other than a low-pitch bruise.

Where else can the captive escape,
if not into a song?

They hold vinyls like steering wheels,
traverse daydreams and desires.
Sing each lyric, breathe each beat.
Angels take off their halos
and use them as tambourines.

Black joy doesn't have to be a rare eclipse,
an underground worship session.
Let it be an open un-trespassed garden,
let it be on Tower Bridge, on the tip of the Shard,
an icing in the chest of the moon.

In this version police still arrive
but they find no one in the record shop.
Only those who worship in the spirit
can see in the spirit.

Freedom of Speech

Their hell has not found us yet.

They roam with it around London, an atlas in their other hand.

Wherever words rise from print to memory, and memory to print,
they target.

They believe it is a God-given right to burn any word that burns
them.

Sabarr Bookshop is on their cluttered hit list, we sense it.

Though we tape the letterbox shut and board up the windows,

we find air elsewhere. Before we open a book,

we massage each other's hands to remind us of benign heat.

Some days we open the books just to take in the waft of almond oil

mixed with their pages' decay.

We are all dying anyway, we say to each other with a light laugh.

Those who target us seem to have no clue of their vanity:

eager to create their own hell they forget the real one awaits them.

And so what if their fire hunts this whole place down?

If we die, the books will teach others how to resurrect us.

And if the books die, we have mastered the gift of resurrecting them.

Death has no dominion.

Hell hath fury. But havens birth an immortal kind of blackness.

Our Appellations: Orúkọ Àbíkú

This is to say you walked into the room
while we were collapsing stars
making black holes for burials.
We screamed at your appearance.
You looked nothing like the one who just died,
but we were desperate for resurrection.
We called you Kusaanu (for death had mercy).
No one could hear your wails above theirs.
In your old age, when your lover asks
why you're leaving suddenly,
you'll tell them you are tired of staying
as a favour, not out of desire.

Laugh with Me

run for shelter, friend,
run for shelter

    Molara Ogundipe-Leslie, 'Yoruba Love'

Elder, laugh with me:
I met a man.
His hands are two lanes of safety.
Professor Molara Ogundipe
I travelled here from your words.
You remain alive in my memory,
wearing your purple dress,
earrings dangling
as you told the workmen
to quieten their bulldozers
so we could hear each other.
We laughed that afternoon
between accounts of strenuous days,
your parables of womanhood.
If you were here,
you would love the man I love.
I imagine us inviting you round,
preparing a table for you.
I would hand you a rubber cast
of my ears as a souvenir.
In the middle of our conversation
our neighbour would start
their raucous lawnmower.
You would open your mouth
about to object this damn bulldozer.

Then I would catch your eye,
my lips spread into a smirk.
We would laugh with our bellies.
All three of us.

Notes from Housewarmings at Mbari

ENTRY 1, 1961

The crack in the wall has stretched itself into a window.
This home delights in being possessed
by the poems we chant in it.

ENTRY 2, 1962

I drew open the curtains. A vision:
children playing dice, the heat a soft backdrop.
Here we swallow the day with soup,
relive and reimagine exits.

ENTRY 3, 1963

Is the power in our poems
or in concentrating them in one setting?
During the reading tonight
the poet's voice made me shiver
like water rediscovering flesh.

ENTRY 4, 1964

Sometimes there are three of us in here,
other times more than twenty-four.
We speak of things,
connect potholes to black holes,
cement to clouds, trace eagles and earlobes,

present scenes of men & women
who tried to fight their maker,
their knuckles bruised from punching heaven's gates.

ENTRY 5, 1965

I have filed copies of my poems
in the same folder which holds my birth certificate.
Both contain our existence in a few words.

ENTRY 6, 1966

No family exists without pet names.
Mine is Citizen of Stubbornness.
I gladly brush my goat hairs.
Even if we opted to be quiet poets
our voices would still emerge
louder than a convoy of sirens.

ENTRY 7, 1967

We walk our own lives in different lands,
but I know we are the same.
I can see it in the tick of our mouths,
in the way we laugh
as we pull flags like tubers from the ground.

It is 3 a.m. and we have been here days in a row.
We shall hold the night hostage.
Butter the African moon onto our plates.

In Praise of Fourteen Years of Friendship

Here we are, liquid dolphins at a salsa bar
in Charing Cross, diving backwards in red dresses,
crushing on our instructors. Here we are
same day as last year, like the year before, and
before, chewing on caked calendars,
renewing the various verbs of friendship.
Here we are splitting the Uber on the way home,
from dinner, from uni, crazy golf, big bake, barbeque,
Little Simz' 'Woman' plays – your laugh is an aux cord.
Here we are in the quiet, tending to the bell-less cows,
that job we hate, the footprint of our failures,
the future we are hiking towards.
Who are we without gathered memories? Just two girls
in a restaurant bathroom asking where the queue starts.

How to Make Your Own National Cake

In the tiny kitchen friends offload cashews from a sack.
They were planted by the most patient among them.

The pragmatic friend plugs in their food processor;
grinds the cashews into a flour, tender and gritty

as the days have been. The brisk friend has a bowl ready,
creams the butter and sugar, chest light with excitement.

The everything-is-a-joke friend brought the eggs used
in yesterday's egg spoon race; whisks them in.

Afterwards, the contents are scooped into the bowl of flour.
The calm friend, the one attentive to the act of breathing

and rising, adds a dash of baking powder,
then stirs the spatula into the mix of soft waves.

The batter is poured into a baking tin and put in the oven.
The friends gather and wait for the cake to cool.

The creative friend cuts the cake into a curious shape,
spreads yellow icing, beautifies it for the eye.

The friends share the cake among themselves,
years of dense dreams soften in their mouths. Relief.

The industrious friend surveys the masses this will save,
considers the value of baking in bulk.

The visionary friend speaks of creamy lands,
of purpose-filled jobs, of dignified stomachs.

The friends leave some cake untouched.
They know

the nation whose party never made them guests
will demand a friendly chunk.

Situationship

What are we? you ask.
He says I am . . . and you are . . .
But what are *we* together? you ask.
He says labels irritate his skin;
he needs a patch test first.

But when we reach the shore,
how should others address *us*?
They want to know, too, you say.
He smiles, skates his tongue over teeth.
He says, When that time comes

they will be dazzled by the answer.
And oh! did you know that most ships
are named after women? he asks.
Then hands you a paper boat.
He is a master of gifts.

You cleave to the folds.
This is why when you hear
the roving song of the ocean
you think nothing of it.
Until water barges into your lungs.

You scramble for the top
of the paper boat, but the sides
are steeper than you remember
they tip you back
before you can catch some air

You call out for your lover,
then realise he never boarded.
He was just the engineer
who made this sinking boat for you.
It even bears your name.

Discernment

In the twenty-first century, in the back seat of a car,
a boy braided a kiss behind my ear.
He read me his stories. All the main characters
had stolen something from me.
I laughed cartooninshly like Bugs Bunny
in the flesh. I loved his surprises.
We made plans for an undated future,
drove in the dark street
where only the moon was our co-conspirer.

> In the thirteenth century Saint Clare of Assisi
> was unable to attend mass.
> God turned her wall into a screen of visions.
> In her room she perceived the service
> in its sensory entirety.

The next morning my mother Clare called me to her room.
The T V by her wall was switched off.
She traced the invisible braid at the back of my ears.
She told me other possible endings for my story.
Claimed no work is finished solely by an author:
some entries are made by corrupted chance.

I reported our talk to the boy and he too shuddered.
New questions consumed us. If we could really see each other,
would we still think ourselves fit to be the other's saviour?

> In the thirteenth century Saint Clare of Assisi refused
> to marry the men that were lined up for her.
> She gave herself to God instead.
> Goodness, what did she see in their eyes?

Mother, O strong-headed hero of sight,
living through the divisions of the flesh and spirit.
I have submitted to the restlessness of youth,
which means I am frustrated
by the walls you urge me to observe.

First Love

Just one last favour – reverse
    back into the empty
    parking bay
    at Tesco's.
Let tyres smudge our former full stop.
    Leave
    the song playing,
    let its stream be cleaned of our litter.
Can you exit
    the car?
    Head over to my side.
    Avoid the windscreen.
I will remain
    sat inside
    sifting our last words
    soothing my sore self.
I want you to unlock my door,
    then close it again,
    careful this time
    not to jam all my five fingers.
Then drive me
    home
    in civil
silence.

Stages of Naming

Out of the ground the Lord God formed every beast of the field and every bird of the air, and brought them to Adam to see what he would call them.

Genesis 2:19

i

And Adam uttered a name, *bird*.
Was pleased with his choice.

ii

Then, he was nudged by a new flock of birds,
Each of varying feather and feature.
Adam pondered, then offered a new layer
of naming, a name within a name,
Nicators. Griffon vulture. Laysan honeycreeper.
They each flew to Adam's arm when called.
Adam must have thought
he had proved his skill at naming:
passed the test of sifting likeness from likeness,
benign beasts from belligerent;
at making each name feel known.

iii

Then Adam slept, clasping his new power.
But he was struck awake by a presence before him.
A likeness unlike any he had ever seen.
Flesh, drawing towards him.
She desired to be named. Adam called her *woman*.
For the first time he explained his reasoning to God.
And woman smiled at him,
spoke back in the way the animals couldn't.
She was not the one who set the test,
but it was she he was now desperate to please.

iv

Then Adam & Woman became familiar with flesh,
ate the only fruit forbidden in their garden.
They forgot there was one still watching.

God cursed them.

Adam, in a panic to protect his wife, called out for her,
Eve!
He paused, startled by this unrehearsed name.
Eve, he repeated, meaning *mother of living things*.
And she lived. Physically, at least.
They both must have gazed at themselves,
overwhelmed by the discovery:
the power of a name to bring beings to life.
The power to stop them from dying.

Bride Price

My parents send photos of themselves eating
my absence for breakfast.
Lips fashioned into smiles.
Twelve tubers of yam are stacked in the kitchen
like logs to build their new life.
Flowers queue on the counter of every window
demanding intense nurture, the way a child does.

When my husband and I visit we sit
on the bags of rice that double as bean bags.
My parents joke about the bride price list,
the things they could have added. They say kola nuts
are too bitter, say we become what we eat
so they were right to leave them out.

The dining is a free market-stall of fruit baskets.
With each squeeze of an orange, a burst
of brightness crosses my mother's face.
And with each peel of a banana
my father rediscovers himself.

My husband and I speak the future tense,
say someday we too will recite the script of parents.
We promise ourselves there is no pressure,
say this as we clench a handful of rice grains over a pot,
pour it slow and slender like sand into an hourglass.

Umbrella

Rere ojú; ojú ni afeni, ṣùtì lehìn. ('Friendship that depends on presence offers friendship in one's presence but despises one when one is absent.')

Yoruba proverb

The term 'best friend' makes me cringe;
too absolute, too naive. 'Close friends' is less severe,
though mathematical. Involves routine measurement
of the closeness between two bodies.
Forgive me, I was engrossed by Maths in school.
You preferred History.
There are slight differences between us.
In school we exist in the same realm,
year after year, but afterwards
we are thrust into different timescapes,
beckoned by the evolving navigators of adulthood.
Come rainstorm or blizzard, I cherish how we try
to remain abreast, to maintain
the stretch of commitment over us.
Life is lifeing we both say
when absence air-kisses us too long.
The clouds above us are rarely the same anymore.
How loud is the silent recovery from temporal angst?
There are no vows for friendship,
but there are terms and conditions in tiny-cursive-letters.
There is the assumption your breath towards mine,
and mine to yours, will be windproof.
Maybe our hands are simply tired of holding
the umbrella term for what we are, 'friends'.
These things happen. And when a downpour comes,
all I wish is for you and me to have a covering.

Moving in with My Husband

The van parks by our flat in SE London.
It's raining, so we put up our hoodies.
We open the communal entrance door,

and are startled by the flooded hallway.
The staircase has been converted into a water fountain.
Where on earth have we based our lives?

My shoes groan at the spit in their mouths.
I slowly walk up two flights of stairs
searching for what ruptures our new home.

At the top, I find that rain is falling from the roof,
strangely, through a small fire alarm.
We race our knuckles along neighbours' doors

but no one opens. Maybe they are away,
or maybe this is a normal occurrence here –
the sky, an indulged guest.

After all our prepping,
it's hard to find our rainboots
among the pyjamas, heels, and frozen apples.

Is this an omen? That our lives will
be a storehouse bursting with wonders?
That the sky itself will avenge us against the fire?

The van driver says new builds these days are weak.
We ignore him. Ponder what we have witnessed
as we wade our wardrobe through the water.

Measuring Light

All that paperwork, legal uniformity.
We swim in the pale pool of history.

We joke that he could have taken mine.
Either way someone surrenders.

I always liked the sound of his surname –
Perhaps it was just instinctive.

My husband and I have now reached
for the physics of being

to find a resolution we can rest in.
We stand before each other,

our faces appear transfigured.
We unveil each other in unison.

By sharing one surname,
we declare we have combined

our individual lights.
We call it concentrated radiance.

A letter has come in
addressed to Mr & Mrs———.

I smile, & light, so much of it, pours out
of my body, to the table, floor,

even flows out from under the door.
This pool is glistening.

I see it, know it, feel it.
We swim in it.

Our Appellations: Orúkọ Inagijẹ

When you're eighty with silver candy hair,
I'll still call you *Melon*.
Remember how on Sunday afternoons
I bring you egusi soup: a drapery of leaves
thickened with ground melon seeds.
Look at your mouth doing *mu e mu e*.
You pull me in, paste your lips on my chest.

Master of Ceremonies

Welcome this conspicuous lady

to the stage.

Welcome, poet
(so terse and inappropriate a word to use)
to the stage.

Welcome, spoken word artist
(that sounds exciting, good for her)
to the stage.

Welcome – (pause) slam poet.
(There's an inside joke of slam as a verb not as a noun)
as she flamingos to the stage.

Welcome, nationwide spokesperson
(she has too many followers who cult her words)
to this stage.

Welcome, *rapper*?
(Ha! apologies I saw one video
where she employed rhythm
on the stage.)

Welcome, this *sweet* woman
(motivational silencer of real poetry)
sneaking her way to this stage.

Welcome, bestseller
(she has been commissioned, not by God,
but by commerce) to the stage.

Where is she? Is she here yet? Is anyone there? Anyone?

Oh goodness, I didn't expect to improvise at this stage.

Owambe Live Band Leader

Celebrate. Celebrate. Celebrate. Celebrate.
Hips, arms, legs, hooray. We wish you long life
today.

Help me greet mummy mummy. Salute
daddy daddy. This one is for sugar sugar.
Lets celebrate proper proper.

This one is for Mr Indoor sunglasses wearer.
Gentleman galore. Mr Sunglasses.
Gentleman galore. Mr Sunglasses.

This one is for the bride. Peperempe.
Sophisticated stride. Peperempe.
You are his night's shining charmer.
                    Peperempe.

Now listen to the talking drum,
its stick like a stethoscope split at the centre
relaying the call of your dinging heart.

I can see all the swimming shoulders,
the lake of one-dollar notes.
Keep coming. Keep coming.

Look at this baby, jumping jumping.
The womb is a fruit we like plucking plucking.

Over the back, I hail you, president of enjoyment
swallowing a third term at the buffet.
We await your presence.

Now listen to the guitar, steel hustling.
Shake the water in your body.
Forget the world. Forget the curfew charge.

What if we just keep dancing, till
God calls us backstage to another stage?
Don't forget heaven has a tighter guest list.
Celebrate. Celebrate. Celebrate. Celebrate.

Wrestling with God

So [God] said to him, 'What is your name?'
He said, 'Jacob'.

When the days collapse
and the sun is fasting from your face,
you bow with grey-moon flesh
to plead – *God, it's me* . . .
there's a name of yours you utter reflexively.
The name that knows the weight
of your hefty spirit.
A listener to your tossing thoughts.
A name that makes you sigh
at its resilience.
The name God catches
your attention with
when he wants to offer you peace.
The kind the world can't give.

Wrestling with God | 75

To My Previous Self

Fizzy-eyed young one, don't judge me.
Don't look so dazed with disappointment,
hands dangling from your bright blue dungarees.
I'm still doing the thing you love,
though I miss loving it the way you did.
        How did you do it?
Climbing skyscrapers in hand-made kits,
wire-walking between clouds,
treating rejection as a bridge.

I have been dreaming about you.
Each time you are slapping my shoulder &
telling me to wake up.
The Yoruba proverb warns of
A-jí-má-boójú: ti nfi ojú àná woran
        A-person who-rises-in-the-morning-without-washing-his-
    face: one who sees things with yesterday's eyes.

Starting today I will exfoliate my regrets.
I will only knock on doors
that have odd numbers – dare me –
even ones that have none.
I will no longer be a tenant of fear.

I am reclaiming that un-choreographable desire I had.
Which means I must swig the air into my throat
and breathe it back into the world newly
effervescent.

The Dream in Which There Is Dancing

I saw my grandfather in a dream
dancing, hands raising his agbada,
swaying, legs swinging.
He was in his home
with familiar and unfamiliar walls
as dreams often have.
Large vases of jute leaves flanked the door.
The air, held by the strong scent of locust beans.
The houses my grandfather owned
were shared sweet as clementine
between his children.
Almost all of us grandchildren
were given his name,
his first becoming our second, third, and fourth.
We have kept it.
For some, it's an heirloom
encased for public view.
How does a man keep his name clean
without his faults crushing it at the root?
I saw my grandfather in a dream dancing,
so I put a leg forward to dance with him.
I want to tell him I too dance through the world,
but differently from him:
I glide my hands on pages, sketch reimaginations.
I called my grandfather's name, but I woke up.
My conscious body was greedy to reunite,
but my subconscious thought I was calling myself.
At first, I was indignant. I couldn't reach him.
Then I realised
this is what descendants pray for.
I am painting my father's father's house
with my own fragrance.

Our Appellations: Orúkọ Oríkì

Henceforth, I'll sing my own name,
let it spring from my mouth,
stretch it into a long string of phrases,
listen out for the harmony of echoes.
I'll dance like the future is watching.

ACKNOWLEDGEMENTS

Thank you, Jesus. Thank you to *Mslexia* magazine for publishing an earlier version of 'My Name Is My Home'. Thank you to Peter Khan and Dami Ajayi for reading my work, and for the insightful conversations.

The journey has required many leaps, and I am grateful for the encouragement of Bernardine Evaristo and Lisette Verhagen.

I extend by deepest thanks to my editors and the Penguin team for their time and care throughout the process of creating this book.

I owe a great deal to my parents for always championing me, and for aiding my research for this book. To my siblings, you both inspire me and your support means the world. Thank you to my dear friends for laughter and warm shoulders. To my love, Tomisin, for everything, just writing your name makes my face light up.

The following sources proved especially helpful: the book's epigraph is taken from Niyi Osundare's essay, 'Yoruba Thought, English Words: A Poet's Journey Through the Tunnel of Two Tongues', in *Thread in the Loom: Essays on African Literature and Culture* (Africa World Press, 2002), pp. 115–31.

The Yoruba proverb which provided the epigraph for 'My Name Is My Home' is from C. L. Adeoye's book, *Oruko Yoruba* (Ibadan: Ibadan University Press, 1982), p. 2.

The italicized words in 'Nocturnal Migrant' are lyrics taken from 'Who Are You?' By Chip.

The epigraph for 'Laugh with Me' is from Molara Ogundipe-Leslie's poem 'Yoruba Love', from her collection *Sew the Old Days and Other Poems* (Ibadan, Evans Brothers, 1985), p. 22.

The epigraphs from 'Umbrella' and 'To My Previous Self' are from Oyekan Owomoyela's book *Yoruba Proverbs* (Lincoln and London: University of Nebraska Press, 2005), pp. 338 and 102.